How to be a Victorian

in 16 easy stages

Contents

Written and illustrated by Scoular Anderson

Know your queen

In Kensington Palace in London on the 20th June 1837, Princess Victoria was woken by the arrival of the Archbishop of Canterbury and the **Lord Chamberlain**. They had come with important news.

When the young princess came out of the bedroom, the Lord Chamberlain went down on one knee and said ...

Your uncle, King William IV, has died. As you are next in line to the throne of Britain, you are now Queen.

Victoria put out her hand to be kissed by the Lord Chamberlain. She was only 18, but she was going to reign for 63 years.

The people had high hopes for Victoria as their queen because the last three monarchs had not been very good.

George III had several bouts of madness.

George IV loved to spend money - especially on food.

William IV was quite old and nicknamed Silly Billy.

People were impressed by the young queen. She took her duties seriously and didn't seem nervous. She spoke in a quiet but clear voice and had an excellent memory.

She looked ordinary and was quite small. If you were walking in the street and her carriage passed by, you might have had difficulty seeing her!

About a year before she became queen, Victoria met Prince Albert of Saxe-Coburg (in Germany). He made a very strong impression on the princess and four years later they were married.

If you lived in London, you might have gone to catch a glimpse of the couple at their wedding. They were married in the chapel at St James's Palace but it wasn't a very grand affair. They left for their honeymoon at Windsor Castle in a shabby old carriage. However, they had a large escort of people in coaches and on horses who travelled on either side of the royal carriage all the way to Windsor.

They were very much in love – though Albert had to put up with Victoria's temper when she chased him from room to room, shouting at him.

Albert did as much as he could to help his wife in her official duties. He had a desk put next to Victoria's so he could help her with all the government documents she had to sign.

Many people thought Albert was a dull, boring man but he was shy and quiet. He was also clever and artistic. As he was not king he had no royal duties, so he looked around for things to do. He came up with a plan for how to run the palace and the queen's **estates** more efficiently. He also designed new helmets for the Household Cavalry.

Sometimes the royal family felt the need to get away from official duties, so Albert designed a holiday home for them on the Isle of Wight. It was called Osborne House.

If you were an artist you might have been invited to paint the royal family at Osborne House. These paintings were so popular that prints were made of them for people to hang up at home.

In 1842, Victoria and Albert travelled north to Scotland for a holiday in the Highlands. The mountains reminded Albert of his home in Germany. The couple liked the place so much they bought an estate called Balmoral and built a holiday home there.

At Balmoral, Albert liked to shoot and fish while Victoria took long walks – sometimes lasting for four hours!

Victoria and Albert settled into family life and had nine children.

Have a great day out

If you were a Victorian you might have visited Prince Albert's biggest idea – the Crystal Palace. This was the nickname given to a huge glass building in Hyde Park, London, designed by Joseph Paxton. On display inside was the Great Exhibition of the works of **industry** of all nations. The exhibition was opened in 1851 by Queen Victoria and was a smash hit. The Queen herself visited every day for several weeks.

Six million people came from all over the country to see the amazing displays of objects. Acrobats on trapezes performed in the central court and organists gave musical concerts. If you were hungry there were plenty of restaurants and cafes. You would like these if you were a young person because you could go and meet friends there without your parents watching over you all the time.

The exhibition made a **profit** which was used to build the Science and Natural History Museums in London.

There were about 100,000 objects on display, just about everything from furniture...

...to false teeth...

...and from machines...   ...to model boats.

Squeeze into bed

Many great changes took place during Victorian times like new inventions, faster transport, better health care and education. These made many people's lives easier and more comfortable.

However, if you were a very poor person, life was hard. Most likely you lived in one of the many old buildings which were built very close together and in need of repair. Perhaps you lived in one of the small houses that were built in rows. You didn't have a garden or any green space nearby.

A street musician plays for the locals. ↓

clothes were washed in tubs, then dried on lines between buildings. ↙

10

None of the houses in your street had plumbing so you had to collect water from a pipe in the street. You had to share the same toilet with several other families. The toilet was usually a hole in the ground in a shed.

Each house had a coal fire. The smoke from all these fires as well as the factory chimneys made the air smoky and **polluted**. Household rubbish was thrown out into the street because no one came to collect it. Families were big – as many as eight or ten children – and several families might share one house. Because of these reasons, many people died young.

Sewage ran through the streets.
↓

There wasn't much furniture in poor homes. There was usually a table with some chairs, stools and a cupboard. You would have to share a bed with several other members of the family. Often this bed was just a mattress stuffed with straw laid on the floor.

If you were a poor person you probably never learnt to cook as you didn't have food that needed much cooking. Most meals were bread with butter or margarine and tea (no sugar or milk). Sometimes flour was mixed with water into a sticky porridge. Some days there was bacon and potatoes. If you earned a bit more money, you could afford some meat, vegetables and perhaps an apple tart as a treat.

Most people in the country lived in houses owned by wealthy landowners. It was up to the landowners to keep these houses in good repair but often they didn't, so the houses were old, damp and uncomfortable. However, at least the air was fresher than in the towns and cities and there were usually gardens around the houses to grow fruit and vegetables.

thatch - roof covering made of straw or reeds

firewood

toilet

vegetables

pigs

hens

Ring for the maid

If you owned a business like a big factory or a shipping company, or if you were the director of a bank, you had a large amount of money. You liked to show off your wealth by building a huge house in the country surrounded by parkland. You probably had a house in the city as well.

main house

garden

If you were rich you had a carriage with a coachman to drive you around. By the end of Victorian times, cars had been invented so you swapped your coachman for a **chauffeur**.

coachman

chauffeur

stables where horses and coaches were kept

glasshouses for growing peaches, apricots and grapes

head gardener's cottage →

Many big houses had walled gardens. The walls protected the plants inside. The head gardener and his team had to provide the big house with fruit, vegetables and flowers throughout the year.

If you were rich you had an army of servants in the house to look after you. They were known as the "below stairs" staff as the rooms where they worked – like kitchens, store rooms or offices – were usually in the basement.

If you were a servant you would find the work was hard and the pay was low – but you had a bedroom and meals were free. If you were young you got the dirtiest jobs – like cleaning out the fires every morning or washing the dishes, pots and pans. If you were lucky and worked hard you might get **promotion** and end up as a butler or housekeeper.

The butler was in charge of running the household and the male staff. He organised the serving of meals.

The housekeeper looked after the female staff and the household cleaning.

The cook was in charge of kitchen staff and cooking of meals.

Footmen served meals, kept the fires burning and cleaned the silver.

The scullery maid prepared vegetables, washed up dishes and generally helped the cook.

Housemaids did all the cleaning. They started at 6 a.m. and didn't finish until 10.30 p.m.

There was a group of people in Victorian times who were neither very poor nor very rich. They were called the middle classes – like doctors, lawyers and shop owners. Their houses were not as grand as those of the very rich and were often joined together in a row called a terrace.

If you were a middle-class person your house usually had a drawing room (a best room for meeting guests), a parlour (family sitting room), a dining room and two or three bedrooms. You might have a nursery for your children on the top floor. If you were a middle-class family you might not be able to afford a carriage but you probably had a cook and at least one maid.

The middle classes preferred to live at the edge of cities and towns away from the smoke and smells. They had to **commute** into the city centre to work.

Clutter up your rooms

If you were a rich or middle-class Victorian, you liked to have lots of clutter in your rooms. You probably had an over-mantle on top of your fireplace. This was a mirror surrounded by little shelves to display your knick-knacks and souvenirs. Chairs were comfy and windows were draped with thick curtains.

armchair

a whatnot

a sewing table

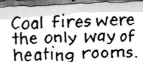

Coal fires were the only way of heating rooms.

The Victorians believed that plants helped to clean the air, so rooms had lots of plants in pots.

In the past, **dyes** for fabrics had come from plants. In Victorian times, **chemical** dyes were invented which gave rich, bright colours. The new colours were used in carpets, curtains, chair covers and wallpaper.

Victorians liked to have lots of pictures on their walls. If you were rich, you had family portraits painted. Other people bought framed prints. Poor people liked to cut pictures from magazines and paste them to the walls.

At the start of Victorian times, houses didn't have bathrooms. If you were a rich or middle-class Victorian, a maid carried hot water all the way up from the kitchen to a metal bath which was placed in the middle of the bedroom. A maid would have to empty your potty, too!

By the end of Victorian times, plumbing was better. There were baths with water from taps and flushing toilets had been invented.

A commode– where you kept your potty!

wash stand where you washed yourself in the morning

STAGE 6

Pop out for a sandwich

If you were a Victorian you knew all about "takeaway" food.
Many poor people had no proper kitchens, so they had no way
of cooking at home. It was easier to eat food from street stalls.
Some of the things you could buy were soup and shellfish,
oranges and apples, hot chestnuts, pies of all kinds, cakes
and sandwiches. Ginger ale and lemonade were popular drinks.

There were
coffee stalls
in every street.
↓

There were no disposable cups so
you drank your coffee at the stall
and handed back your cup and
saucer. ↓

A coster girl
sold fruit. ↓

Apples! Apples!

Boiled eggs

Ham
sandwiches

Coffee

People didn't drink water as it was usually polluted. Food was often polluted, too. Stallholders added things to food so there was a bit more to sell and they earned more money. Water was added to milk, as well as chalk to make it look whiter. Sand was put into sugar and ground acorns into coffee. Sometimes floor sweepings were put into tea and ground bones into bread!

By the end of Victorian times, inventors had discovered how to keep food fresh in cans. The invention of ice-making machines meant that cheaper meat and fish could be brought from far-off places like Australia and Canada.

Try a curtsey in a crinoline

If you were a woman in Victorian times you wore a long dress which reached right to the ground. It had a tight waist and was decorated with lots of bows, buttons and frills. As fashion changed, dresses got wider and wider. The dresses were made up of so much material they had to be held up by a frame of metal and tape. This was known as a crinoline.

You usually needed help to get into a crinoline. It was difficult to wear- especially in high winds!

A short coat called a mantelet was worn over the dress.

In the middle of Victorian times, dresses began to shrink again. Lots of material was pulled to the back of the dress and this was called a bustle.

By the end of Victorian times dresses became narrower and more comfortable to wear.

The Queen herself wasn't very fashionable and wore wide dresses to the end of her life.

Poorer women never wore crinolines or bright colours. They wrapped themselves in shawls to keep warm and pulled the shawl over their heads when they were in the street.

Both men and women wore hats when they went outdoors and older women often wore lace caps indoors.

boots and shawl for a working woman

Victorian ladies didn't use many **cosmetics** – perhaps just a little rouge to make their cheeks pink. Queen Victoria thought wearing make-up was a horrible habit. It was fashionable for rich and middle-class ladies to keep their skin as pale as possible. They always took **parasols** when they went out on sunny days and closed the curtains if the sun shone indoors.

If you were a fashionable young Victorian man, you liked to show off with bright clothes. As there was no central heating in homes or offices, you wore thick underwear all year.

By the end of Victorian times, fashion changed and men wore clothes in shades of black or grey.

waistcoat with wild pattern

sky-blue jacket

yellow trousers

orange gloves

Men wore their hair long – just over the ears or down to the collar. A fashionable hairstyle was to part hair in the middle and brush the sides forwards. Men also grew their side whiskers very long and these were known as "dundrearies". By the end of Victorian times hair was cut short.

If you were a poor Victorian child, you might have had to go around without shoes. Clothes were often handed down from the oldest to the youngest.

Top hats were very fashionable and even poor lads would wear one if they could.

If you were a rich Victorian child, you had to dress smartly at all times. Children's clothes were very like adults' but girls' skirts were shorter.

cape

hat with feather

boots

suit with short trousers

long boots

Take out the toybox

Family life was important to the Victorians. Apart from in poor families, husbands went out to work while wives looked after the home.

If you were a child from a rich family, you were treated quite strictly and you had to be polite and **obedient**. You probably had a **nanny** to look after you. You spent most of your time in the nursery. This was a room where you played, ate your meals and sometimes did your lessons.

Poor children in the country and towns played out of doors.

If you were a rich Victorian child you played with plenty of toys. There were board games like Snakes and Ladders and Ludo. There were beautiful dolls dressed in the latest fashions. Clockwork toys made of metal were popular – especially train sets.

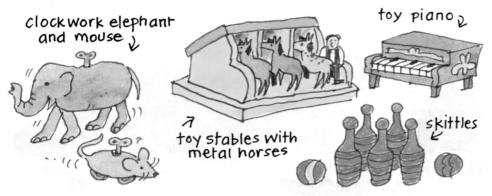

clockwork elephant and mouse ↓

toy stables with metal horses ↗

toy piano ↓

skittles ↙

Poor children played with home-made toys. Sometimes they could buy a cheap toy from a "penny stall" or the "chapman" – a man who came round country villages selling toys, ribbons and knick-knacks.

You threw the spinning diabolo ← into the air then caught it on the string.

27

Scratch in the sand

At the beginning of Victorian times, children didn't have to go to school – so many of them couldn't read or write. Unlike rich children, poor children didn't go to school because they worked to earn money for their family.

At some schools you had to pay for the lessons – only a few pence – but many families couldn't afford it.

blackboard ↘

cane ←

Some schools were run by a church or a charity. A "dame school" was run by a single lady in her own home.

If you were a rich boy, you might go to an expensive **public school**.
You were expected to go to university when you left school. Girls from rich families were usually taught at home by a **governess**.

In the middle of Victoria's reign, the government passed a law called the Education Act which meant all children had to go to school between the ages of five and 13.

If you were a pupil in a Victorian school, you sat at desks which were set out in rows facing the teacher. You had to behave or you felt the teacher's **cane** on your hand or back.

Often, facts were learnt by chanting them over and over again...

Two fours are eight.

Two fours are eight.

Two fours are eight. Two...

Pupils wrote with chalk on pieces of **slate** or traced out letters in a tray of sand.

abacus - to help with counting

When the weather was good you went outside for "drill" – physical exercises to keep you fit.

29

Read all about it

More and more people learnt to read in Victorian times, so reading became a popular pastime.

paperboy selling papers

In the past, printing machines were worked by hand, but in Victorian times steam-driven presses were invented. This meant newspapers were printed quickly and cheaply. People read papers like *The Times*, the *Daily Mail* and the *Telegraph*.

If you were a woman, there were all sorts of magazines with handy tips on how to run your home, fashion articles and adverts for the latest gadgets.

If you were a teenager you looked out for the latest "penny-dreadful". These were magazines full of scary stories or romantic adventures. There were magazines with poems, puzzles and competitions. Children read comic books with strip cartoons.

The *London Illustrated News* was one of the most popular newspapers. This was because it was filled with illustrations. Reporters called "specials" were sent off to every corner of the world to get good stories. The fast ships and railways of Victorian times meant they could travel quicker than ever before. They made drawings of important events like battles, shipwrecks or festivals in distant countries. Their sketches were sent back home as quickly as possible, where other artists turned them into illustrations for the newspaper. Readers liked these pictures so much they often had them framed to hang on their walls.

Photography was invented during Victorian times. This meant that reporters could take a picture, which was quicker than doing a drawing.

Equipment was big and heavy, though!

If you were a Victorian who liked reading but couldn't afford books you could pop down to your local library. Public libraries were built in every town and they were open to all.

One of the most popular Victorian authors was Charles Dickens. He had his novels published in magazines chapter by chapter, which got readers hooked. They couldn't wait for the latest edition to find out what happened next!

Other popular novels were written by three sisters, Charlotte, Anne and Emily Brontë. However, in Victorian times it wasn't thought proper for women to write books, so the Brontës had to invent men's names for themselves.

Charles Dickens gave readings of his novels to large audiences.

There were plenty of books for children, too. If you wanted adventure you read books like *Treasure Island* by Robert Louis Stevenson. The most popular book of all was *Alice's Adventures in Wonderland* by Lewis Carroll.

Make sure you're up on time

For hundreds of years most people lived in the countryside in villages or small towns. They worked for the landowners on their farms or had other trades like **thatching**, **blacksmithing** or basket making.

Many people made a living weaving cloth in their homes.

Woman spinning thread for weaving

In Victorian times all that changed. Machines were invented which made things quicker than making them by hand – especially cloth. Huge factories were built in towns and cities and filled with these machines. Steam-driven farm machinery put many farm workers out of a job, so if you were a poor country Victorian, the chances are you moved to the nearest big city to find work in a factory. You hoped for a better life and more money. By the end of Victoria's reign, most people lived in cities.

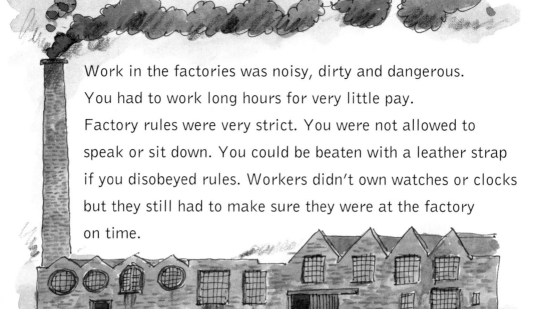

Work in the factories was noisy, dirty and dangerous. You had to work long hours for very little pay. Factory rules were very strict. You were not allowed to speak or sit down. You could be beaten with a leather strap if you disobeyed rules. Workers didn't own watches or clocks but they still had to make sure they were at the factory on time.

Children as young as four worked alongside adults. "Scavengers" were children who had to crawl under weaving machines to pick up bits of thread. They were often badly injured by the whirling machinery.

Many wealthy people were shocked by the hardships of the poor and tried to help. Lord Shaftesbury was a politician who got parliament to pass the Factory Act in 1833. This banned children from working in mines and limited the time children worked in factories to ten hours a day.

A factory owner called Robert Owen wanted to make life better for his workers. The cotton-spinning factory he built at New Lanark had comfortable houses, gardens, a school, a church and health care for when people fell ill.

If you didn't work in a factory there were other things you could do to earn money.

pieman

flower seller →

shoe-shine boy

horse-manure ← collector

If you were a young middle-class man, most likely you worked in a counting house, which was an office.

In Victorian times documents had to be copied by hand and pages of numbers added up in your head. You sat at a high desk all day. If you were unlucky enough to be far away from the only fire, you wore your scarf and gloves!

If you were a Victorian woman, you were expected to get married and become a housewife, but some women worked as shop assistants or governesses, looking after young children. However, typewriters were invented at the end of Victorian times and offices began to fill up with women because it was thought they were better than men at using typewriters.

Catch the 4.32

If you wanted to go on a long journey at the start of Victorian times, you took a **stagecoach**. Travel by coach was not very comfortable and took a long time. Roads were muddy and full of potholes. Lots of things could go wrong – horses went **lame**, wheels came off and sometimes coaches overturned.

Longer journeys took several days, so you had to stop and stay the night at inns along the way.

During Victoria's reign, travel began to change. Engineers were trying to invent a machine that would move around powered by steam. These machines would replace horses and could pull carts much faster along metal rails. The most successful engineer was George Stephenson, helped by his son Robert. They built a railway engine they called Locomotion No.1.

On its first trial run, it pulled carts filled with coal and sacks of flour 24 kilometres in 2 hours – an amazing speed in those days. Not long after this, a wooden carriage filled with people was pulled by the engine. It was the first passenger train to run on a railway. Within 30 years, railways had spread to every corner of the country.

To begin with, train journeys weren't very comfortable. If you couldn't afford first class you had to stand in an open carriage and get covered in smoke and soot from the engine.

The railways completely changed people's lives. If you were a Victorian you could take a train and travel far from home quite cheaply. Farmers got vegetables, milk and meat to markets and cities quickly. People far from the sea could buy fish on the day it was caught. Letters and newspapers were delivered to towns along the railway lines in a few hours.

Stagecoaches still ran for a while but began to die out. Horses were used for short journeys in carts or for pulling big vehicles like fire engines, ambulances or removal vans.

Wealthy people owned a carriage to get them around. If you didn't have a carriage, you could hire a hansom cab (Hansom was the name of the inventor). Cabs were like taxis today and the streets were full of them.

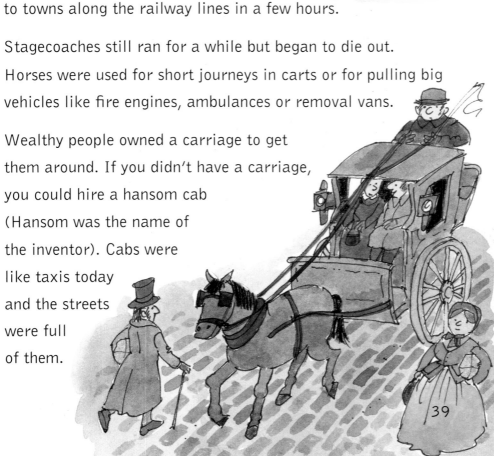

If you were late for work, you might jump on an omnibus. These vehicles appeared on the city streets in Victorian times. The word omnibus means "for all" and was soon shortened to bus. They ran along set routes in the cities. You could squeeze inside or climb up the narrow ladder to sit on seats on the roof.

Many people couldn't even afford an omnibus so walking was common.

JAMES RONIN & SONS   WORLDWIDE REMOVERS

EAGLE AVENUE - SPARROW LANE - HAWK STREET.

Towards the end of Victorian times another invention appeared which became very popular. If you were a Victorian who couldn't afford a carriage or bus travel, then the bicycle made life easier. You could go places very cheaply on a bicycle. It gave people great freedom, especially women. They usually had to have a man with them, but they could go off on their own if they were riding a bicycle.

The first bicycles that were invented had no pedals.

At the end of Victoria's reign, cars appeared on the streets. Harry J. Lawson opened the first factory to build cars in Britain. It was called the Daimler Motor Company.

Early cars had no roofs.

41

Get some fresh air

During Victorian times the government passed a law which put a limit on the number of hours people had to work, so people had more **leisure** time. The government also created special days called "bank holidays" which gave people several extra days' holiday.

Sports like football, cricket, rugby and tennis had been played for a long time but they became very popular in Victorian times. If you were a member of a sports team, you could now travel to a distant town to play an away match – thanks to the railways.

For women, playing tennis in Victorian clothes wasn't easy!

Victorian football kit ↘

The seaside became a favourite place to visit. If you were a Victorian on a day out, you wore your very best clothes. The Victorians kept most of their bodies covered and it was not polite to take off any clothes – no matter how hot it was.

Promenades were built in seaside towns so that people could stroll along without getting sand in their shoes. Iron piers were built so people could walk out to sea and breathe the fresh, salty air.

pleasure steamer

postcards and souvenirs being sold →

At the seaside children could watch a Punch and Judy puppet show, ride a donkey, or be pulled in a cart by a goat.

You could take a dip in the sea but you had to wear a costume that covered all of your body. You changed clothes in a hut on wheels which was pulled down to the water's edge to give you as much privacy as possible.

Enjoy paintings and pianos

Rich people were always able to buy paintings to hang on their walls at home. However, if you were a Victorian who couldn't afford paintings but liked looking at them, you were in luck. Art galleries began to appear in Victorian cities, where you could go and see paintings for free. Victorian artists liked to paint pictures that told a story. They also liked to paint large pictures full of detail.

If you were a rich or middle-class Victorian, making music at home was a popular pastime. Families gathered round the piano in the evenings for a good old sing-song.

You could go out and enjoy yourself by watching a famous actor in a play at the theatre. Victorians were fond of **opera** or very grand pieces of music played by large orchestras and choirs.

If you wanted a bit of a laugh you went to a music hall to see a variety show. There would be dancers and singers who sang your favourite songs. There were also magicians, comedians and acrobats.

STAGE 15

Be amazed by the big and the new

If you were a Victorian walking round the streets of a town or city, you might notice lots of building work going on. The Victorians built many new houses but also public buildings like libraries, museums, churches and railway stations. The Victorians liked these buildings to be very grand. They were fond of a style from the Middle Ages called Gothic. This meant buildings had pointed windows, doors and spires and lots of decoration.

Gothic-style church ↘

Victorians used bricks of various colours to make patterns on walls of buildings.

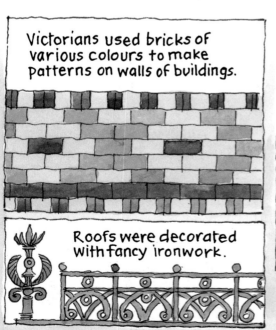

Roofs were decorated with fancy ironwork.

Windows were surrounded by fancy woodwork called "barge boarding".

47

It wasn't just Victorian architecture that was very grand –
their engineering projects were spectacular too. The Forth
Rail Bridge was the first structure in Britain to be made
of steel. It was started in 1883 and took nearly seven years
to complete. It was built to carry the railway line across the
River Forth but it had to be high enough to allow
ships to pass underneath.

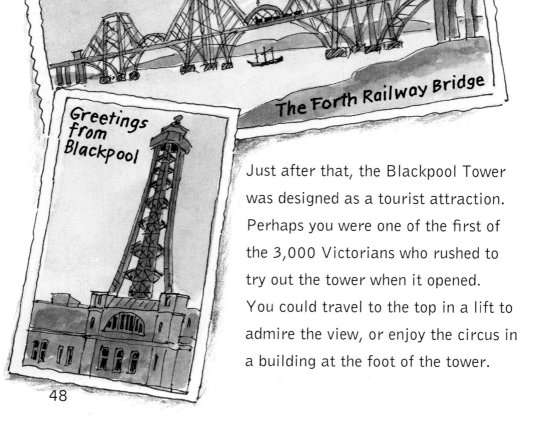

postcard

The Forth Railway Bridge

Greetings
from
Blackpool

Just after that, the Blackpool Tower
was designed as a tourist attraction.
Perhaps you were one of the first of
the 3,000 Victorians who rushed to
try out the tower when it opened.
You could travel to the top in a lift to
admire the view, or enjoy the circus in
a building at the foot of the tower.

48

The Victorian age was a time of great inventions. Many scientists around the world had been trying to invent a machine which would allow people to talk to one another at a great distance. Alexander Graham Bell was the first to come up with an idea that worked – the telephone. Thomas Edison made a better model with a stronger sound.

If you were wealthy you could afford your own telephone. Otherwise you could phone from one of the telephone boxes that began to appear. They were just wooden huts and some of them had attendants who unlocked the hut and took your money!

One of the greatest inventions of the Victorian age was electricity. Cragside, a house in the north of England, was the first place in the world to be lit by electric light bulbs.

After that, lots of electrical inventions appeared...   kettle

iron

cooker

Say goodbye

If you were a Victorian who had become wealthy you could enjoy a good lifestyle with a comfortable home and holidays abroad. Isambard Kingdom Brunel designed the first ship to be powered by propellers. Rich passengers could travel across the Atlantic on holiday in great luxury.

Sadly, there were still many poor people in Victorian Britain. Some of them left to go to other countries like the USA, Canada or Australia in the hope of finding a better life. On the way you would have to put up with cramped conditions, hunger, disease and the risk of shipwreck and pirates.

the rich...

...and the poor

50

Queen Victoria's husband, Prince Albert, died in 1861.
He was only 42 years of age.
Victoria lived for another 40 years, though she never got over Albert's death and wore black clothes for the rest of her life.

a souvenir brooch of the Queen's diamond jubilee

For many years after Albert's death she was not seen much by the public and became unpopular. However, by the time she celebrated her diamond jubilee – 60 years as queen – she had become popular again and people celebrated with street parties throughout the country.

During Victoria's reign great changes had taken place in everyone's life. If you were a child when Victoria became queen, you probably lived in the countryside and it was usual for you to stay in the area where you were born. By the time Victoria died you could travel on a train to any part of the country. Cars had appeared on the roads and the first cinema had opened. Britain's factories, inventions and trade had made it one of the most powerful countries in the world.

Glossary

blacksmithing	making things from iron, using heat and hammers
bouts	periods of illness
cane	a stick for hitting people with
chauffeur	someone whose job is driving a car
chemical	made, rather than found in nature
commute	travel every day
cosmetics	make-up
dyes	substances used to colour fabric
estates	land and houses
governess	a woman teacher who lived with the family who employed her
industry	business and trade
lame	hurt in the foot or leg and unable to walk well
leisure	free from work
Lord Chamberlain	the chief official of the royal household
nanny	a woman who is employed to look after young children at home
obedient	doing what you are told
opera	a play where everything is sung
parasols	umbrellas to keep off the sun
pleasure steamer	a boat with a propeller, which took people on short trips
polluted	full of dirt
profit	more money than it cost to set up the exhibition
promenades	paved public walkways along the seaside
promotion	a job with more money and responsibility
public school	a well-regarded school that charges fees
stagecoach	a horse-drawn coach that travelled on an established route
thatching	making roofs from bundles of straw or reeds

Index

GALLERY OF GREAT VICTORIAN INVENTIONS

THE GREAT EXHIBITION

PHOTOGRAPHY

THE BICYCLE

THE TYPEWRITER

THE PASSENGER TRAIN

ELECTRICITY

THE TELEPHONE

THE PUBLIC LIBRARY

THE MOTOR CAR

Ideas for reading

Linda Pagett B.Ed (hons), M.Ed
Lecturer and Educational Consultant

Learning objectives: appraise a text quickly, deciding on its value, quality or usefulness; sustain engagement with longer texts, use different narrative techniques to engage and entertain reader; use a range of oral techniques to present persuasive arguments

Curriculum links: History

Interest words: blacksmithing, bouts, chapman, chauffeur, commute, cosmetics, crinoline, dundrearies, governess, cavalry, monarch, opera, parasols, profit, promenades, promotion, trapeze, thatching

Resources: whiteboard, writing materials, internet

Getting started

This book can be read over two or more reading sessions.

- Explain that you will be using an information book to research what it was like in Britain over one hundred years ago. Ask children what they think makes a good information book, e.g. helpful images, glossary.

- Invite a child to read the blurb. Encourage children to be critical when they discuss their initial thoughts on the book, prompting them with questions, e.g. *Is this a book you look forward to reading?*

- Using the glossary, make sure that children understand new vocabulary.

Reading and responding

- Demonstrate reading the first few pages aloud and discuss the use of "If you were a" to help readers to imagine they were living in that time. Ask children whether they think this helps them to understand what life was like in Victorian times and how each topic compares to their own life.

- Using the contents pages, give pairs of children chapters to read. Encourage them to read quietly and make notes on the elements that are different from life today, and why. Prompt them to discuss the main points of their chapter within their pairs.

"Yap, yap!"

Yazz barks at me again. "Yap, yap!"

Yazz barks too much.

"Hush, Yazz," I yell.

Yazz has lots of fizz.

Yazz is as quick as a bee.

Zip, zap!

Buzz, buzz!

Yap, yap!

Yazz runs to the yard.

Now Yazz hops up and down.

He barks again.
"Yap! Yap!"

Now I see!

Yazz is looking for food.
Yazz needs his dinner.

Now Yazz gets his food.

Yum yum!

"Woof! Woof!"

Now I am looking for food as well.
I need my dinner too.

Yum yum!

"Woof, woof, Yazz!" I tell him.

This is my dog, Yazz.

Yazz is quick.

Yazz is in such a rush.

Yap, Yap, Yazz

Written by
Stephen Rickard

Illustrated by
Andy Hamilton

Ransom

Yazz zooms into the garden.
He zig-zags up and down.

Can you see him run?